CLB 1521
© Illustrations and text: Colour Library Books Ltd.,
    Guildford, Surrey, England.
Text filmsetting by Acesetters Ltd., Richmond, Surrey, England.
Printed in Spain.
All rights reserved.
1985 edition published by Crescent Books, distributed by Crown Publishers, Inc.
ISBN 0 517 601869
h g f e d c b a

IDITAROD

The 1000 Mile Marathon

BILL HARRIS

CRESCENT BOOKS
NEW YORK

Facing page: a dog team in Anchorage shortly after the start of the Iditarod Trail Race, and (this page) in Settlers Bay.

The first thing you should know about sled dogs is that the way to get them up and going is not to lower your voice to its deepest pitch and say, "on you huskies!" You don't say "mush!" either. What you do is say is largely unprintable.

The myth about "mush" seems to have come down to us from French trappers in Canada who ordered their dogs to "marche!". Ever since, though most commands are a private matter between man and beast, people who drive dog sleds have been called "mushers."

The problem most of them have is not getting their dogs moving, but holding them back. It sometimes takes several husky men to do the job. It's especially true if they are in the Iditarod Trail Race, a punishing run over 1,049 miles between Anchorage and Nome.

If the race were to begin in Miami, where many people would surely agree conditions for spectators, at least, would be a

These pages: Anchorage, backed by the rugged Chugach Mountain Range. This page: a busy 4th Avenue; in March it becomes the official starting point for the gruelling 1,049-mile race.

whole lot pleasanter, the finish line would be somewhere near Pittsburgh.

But it has to start in Anchorage. Tradition demands it, for one thing. It is a tradition that began in 1925, when the city of Nome was threatened by a devastating diptheria epidemic. Nome was snowbound at the time and the only way to get vital serum there was by dogsled from Anchorage, a thousand miles away. A team was sent out from Nenana, a few miles west of Fairbanks, toward Nulato on the Yukon River and one of the era's most famous dog handlers, Leonhart Seppala, left Nome to meet them.

After four days of incredible sledding by anybody's standards, Seppala picked up the serum from a relay team and immediately turned his lead dog, Togo, in the other direction. One day later, he met another team from Nome, handed over the serum and the city was saved. As often happens, some of the credit got lost in the translation and a monument to the event in New York's Central Park lionizes the lead dog Balto, who was at the head of the team that battled a snowstorm over the last several miles. But it's the symbolism that counts and Balto was from Seppala's kennel, though "the Hardy Norseman" considered

him nothing more than a scrub dog. Which says something about the quality of Seppala's kennels.

But Seppala and the others who made the serum run a success have a much better memorial. Alaskans are fond of saying that they have three great events to look forward to each year: Christmas, New Year's and the Iditarod. Of the three, it's safe to say that the race is the most important to most of them. It's easy at any time of the year to get into an argument about dogs. Almost no one talks about Christmas trees or differences among brands of champagne except in December.

The first dog teams were made

up of blue-eyed Siberian Huskies, a breed that has been in Alaska since the earliest Eskimo pioneers. It's hard to imagine that man could improve on these creatures with a head like a wolf and shoulders like a small ox. But the Malamute tribe of Eskimos tried and succeeded in developing a much larger, bulkier and stronger dog. Then, when sled dog racing became a sport around the turn of the century, some mushers found the Siberian too slow and the Malamute too hard to get along with. They began, in a rather unscientific way, to breed a whole new dog, bulky like a Malamute with the endurance of a Siberian, but with the added

quality of speed. The first choice of many for cross-breeding was hounds, which the people who argue about such things say produced an animal without long endurance. Huskies have been mated with whippets and greyhounds, Afghans and Labradors in the quest for speed. And though what many consider a good sled dog still has broad shoulders and almost-white eyes, they are smaller and leaner than their ancestors. They are so different from the traditional Siberian and Malamute breeds, in fact, they have been given a new name: Alaskan Huskies.

Which is best? Drop in at the Board of Trade Saloon on Front Street in Nome. The argument is probably raging there right at this minute.

People in warmer parts of North America got involved in the argument when the great Polar explorations captured the public's fancy in the years before World War I. In those days, though, the argument wasn't over what kind of dogs were best, but whether dogs were best at all. Robert E. Peary, who wrote a self-serving book on "The Secrets Of Polar Travel," said that "the whole difference between (Roald) Amundsen's dash to the South Pole and (Robert) Scott's heroic struggle and tragic finish may be expressed in four letters, *dogs*."

Though he noted that they had all the qualities of the Arctic wolf, including orneriness, and admitted that his men used all sorts of other four-letter words and were often forced to beat the animals to get them to haul sledges loaded with 500 pounds or more some 15 miles a day, he thought the Eskimo's dogs were heaven-sent.

"They require no assistance during the march," he wrote, "and no care or shelter at the camps... With dogs as motors, the food for the men and the fuel for the motors is the same. When a dog is no longer needed, he can be eaten by the party or used for fuel for the other motors and in this way, not an ounce of material is wasted." Amundsen agreed, and after his 1911 dash to the South Pole reported that his men had shot and butchered more than half of the dogs that got him there and assured him a place in history.

Mention that when you drop around at the Board of Trade Saloon. It will start a whole new argument. They may not agree about what breed of dog is best, but in their hearts they love them all.

It is the kind of love that thousands of Americans discovered in 1903, when Jack London's *Call of the Wild* described the love of a man for the great dog, Buck, who had been stolen in California and sold to work in the Yukon gold fields. Almost no boy who has ever shared the adventure can ever forget the day that John Thornton, Buck's human companion, made a bet in Dawson's Eldorado Saloon that the dog could move a thousand pounds

Left and below left: Libby Riddles, winner of the 1985 event.

from a dead standstill. He bet all he had and no reader who had followed the pair through thick and thin could resist an involuntary lurch, as: "Buck threw himself forward, tightening the traces with a jarring lunge. His whole body was gathered compactly together in the tremendous effort, the muscles writhing and knotting like live things under the silky fur. His great chest was low to the ground, his head forward and down, while his feet were flying like mad, the claws scaring the hard-packed snow in parallel grooves. The sled swayed and trembled, half-started forward. One of his feet slipped and one man groaned aloud. Then the sled lurched ahead in what appeared to be a rapid succession of jerks, though it never really came to a dead stop again... half an inch... two inches... The jerks perceptibly diminished as the sled gained momentum, he caught them up, till it was moving steadily along."

And what of the love between man and beast? The tale continues: "Thornton fell on his knees beside Buck. Head against head, and he was shaking him back and forth. Those who hurried up heard him cursing Buck and he cursed him long and fervently, softly and lovingly.

"'Gad, sir! Gad, sir!' spluttered the Snookum Bench King.

'I'll give you a thousand for him sir, a thousand sir – twelve hundred, sir.'

"Thornton rose to his feet. His eyes were wet. The tears were streaming frankly down his face. 'Sir,' he said to the Snookum Bench King, 'no sir. You can go to hell, sir. It's the best I can do for you, sir.'

"Buck seized Thornton's hand in his teeth. Thornton shook him back and forth. As though animated by a common impulse, the onlookers drew back a respectful distance; nor were they ever again indiscreet enough to interrupt."

But that was fiction. To find the same powerful emotion in real life, you need look no further than the Iditarod.

A favorite in the 1982 race, Susan Butcher lost the first place by a margin of three minutes and forty-three seconds after a gruelling sixteen-day journey from Anchorage. (The closest finish of all was in 1978 when Dick Mackey beat Rick Swenson by one second.) But the narrow loss wasn't as hard for Susan to take as the one she felt early in the race when her lead dog, Tekla, had to be sent back.

Tekla had led her to the finish line three times before. "She could read my mind," said Susan, who admitted that the reverse was also true and that the dog's sorrow seemed as great as her own when she was left to be picked up as the rest of the team moved out with another dog, ironically named Copilot, in the lead.

A dog team in Anvik (facing page), a community of some 40 people on the Yukon River, and near Unalakleet on Norton Sound (this page).

Their troubles began when they got lost in a snowstorm along the Yentna River and wound up ten miles off course. Then, adding injury to insult, an accident that dashed the sled into a tree put three of Susan's 15-dog team out of action.

They had to be put aboard the sled, making the sled heavier for the others and putting a special strain on the leader, whose only instinct was to win in spite of the added weight and the 20-mile detour.

Tekla held out for another fifty miles before Susan made the tearful decision to go on without her. "I hated every bone in my body," she said later.

The emotion of leaving an animal behind is one every musher feels at some time, but in the Iditarod everyone knows that a dog left tied to a tree won't be there long and that it will get the kind of attention that might make a hospital nursery jealous. In the Iditarod, everyone gets involved, but the volunteers who are at the receiving end of what is known as the "Dog Drop" are possibly the most unusual. They are inmates at the Hiland Mountain Correctional Center at Eagle River.

When a dog is left behind, the first leg of the trip to the prison courtyard is in any one of a number of small planes that carry them to a variety of airstrips where they are met by other volunteers who load them into portable kennels for a jeep ride the rest of the way. The volunteer inmates keep them and pamper them until they are united with their owners after the race is over. When Tekla was taken there in 1982, she was eventually joined by 300 other sick, tired or injured sled dogs, close to a third of the number that started the race.

It's an event that isn't easy on people, either. Of the 62 people who lined up behind their teams on Front Street in Anchorage for the start of the 1985 race, only 40 reached Front Street in Nome. Among the drop-outs was 67-year-old Joe Redington, Sr., who organized the first Iditarod in 1973 and has raced in all but two. He quit from the 13th when he fell from a six-foot snow drift and cracked a rib. He was on hand for the finish of the race already thinking about the 1986 race.

Why do they do it? There are all sorts of ways to get across Alaska from Anchorage to Nome, and the Iditarod is certainly the hardest. It may also be the most expensive. Though the top prize is $50,000 and the next 19

A snow-swept Shaktoolik, on Norton Sound, and (top right) musher Alan Cheshire, a British contestant, takes a well-earned rest.

finishers share in a $150,000 purse, the entry fee is $1,300 and the care and feeding of the team, added to the cost of gear, comes out to well over $35,000. You can take an around-the-world cruise on the *Queen Elizabeth II* for less.

But the Iditarod is a bigger adventure.

The scenery is the most beautiful in the world if the snow isn't blowing too hard to see it. The race crosses two mountain ranges: the Alaska, where the trail skirts the incredible 20,320-foot Mount McKinley; and the Kuskokwim. It has views of the Kaiyuh Mountains as it runs down along the wide Yukon River and it leads out over the frozen Norton Bay. The trail goes through ghost towns and tiny villages, across lonely passes and empty miles of tundra and the

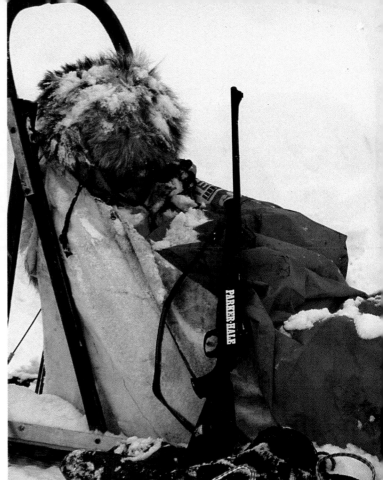

Farewell Burn, more than 350,000 acres of charred rubble left from a two-month forest fire in 1977.

But no one who runs the Iditarod is interested in scenery, except for the markers on the trail. A lot of the time they don't even see those. This is "the last great race." It is a thousand-mile marathon, the kind of experience that delivers a special kind of satisfaction that only runners and other athletes can understand.

Training for it is a year-round responsibility. The dogs are conditioned in the same way marathon runners condition themselves. When there is no snow, they pull wheeled carts. In August, when there is snow in northern Alaska, they are moved to bush towns like Trapper Creek and Clam Gulch where they can get their training with real sleds over the same rough terrain they'll find on the Iditarod Trail. By then, time is short. The race begins during the first week in March.

There is plenty to do in the meantime. Food and supply drops need to be mapped out. Protective clothing needs to be made perfect and the sleds put in mint condition. But not all the contestants have the advantage of living year 'round in Alaska. The 1985 race included a musher from

Ski planes on Iditarod Lake.

A fourteen-dog team on Knik Lake. Top right: an inhabitant of Skwentna, northwest of Anchorage. Bottom right: Joe Redington, one of the founders of the Iditarod Trail Race.

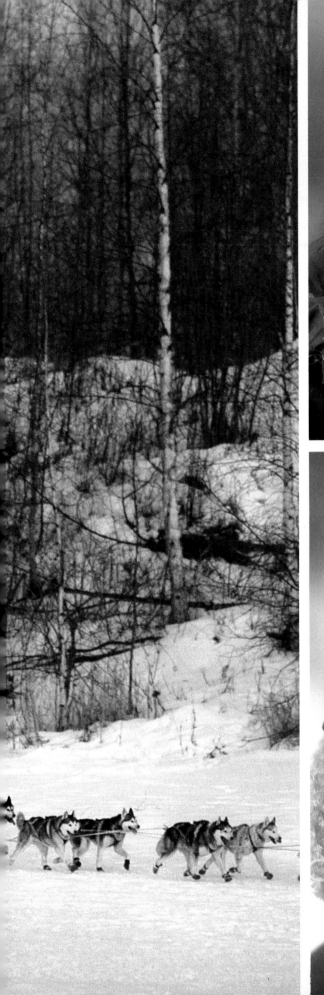

Hawaii. There were three from France and one each from England, Italy, Japan and Australia. If that gives the Iditarod a family resemblence to the Olympic Games, it is only one of the ways. No one who has ever trained for the Olympics has ever trained as hard as anyone with an eye on the Last Great Race.

But international overtones notwithstanding, the Iditarod Trail Race is a uniquely Alaskan institution. "You have to be supertough physically and mentally to run this race," said Joe Redington, and almost no one who takes Alaska seriously doesn't feel that is a good description of their lives. Redington was one of the founders of the race along with a group of local historians. His enthusiasm came from long hours behind a team of dogs rescuing victims of small plane crashes. By the mid 1960s, when even the Royal Canadian Mounted Police abandoned their faithful dogs for faster snowmobiles, it seemed time to do something to preserve the tradition that goes back as far as civilization itself in the North.

Eskimos had done some racing back before the white man came, but it became a popular sport among the sourdoughs Jack London wrote home about during the Yukon Gold Rush in the 1890s. They made heavy bets on the abilities of individual animals as well as teams, but sled dog racing didn't become a serious sport until the first decade of the 20th century with a 400-mile race at Nome, the All-Alaska Sweepstakes.

It has gotten more serious with each passing year and has spread to the lower 48 states. With the spread, the legends have grown. But no race in the more than 75-year history of the sport has made more people aware of dogsledding than the 13th Annual Iditarod Trail Race. It began on Saturday, March 2, 1985 and ended eighteen days, twenty minutes and seventeen seconds later, on Wednesday March 20 at 9:01a.m.

The race itself, stopped twice by bad weather, made history. But the big news was in the outcome. The winner was a woman. Twenty-eight-year-old Libby Riddles took the prize by braving a blizzard that held strong men back. It was an act that came as no surprise to the Alaskans, who don't fight the battle of the sexes in the same way that other Americans do. But it made the rest of the world sit up and take notice.

This page: in Rainy Pass, with the Alaska Mountains in the distance. Facing page: at the ghost-town of Iditarod.

In Alaska, where the two subdivisions of the human species are adults and children, not men and women, some of the excitement came from purists who felt the race may be getting too commercialized. Because the cost of training for it and the running in it is so high, very few mushers can make it to the starting line without the help of dog food companies, thermal clothing makers and others who put up money for some reflected glory in the form of banners and shoulder patches. But Libby Riddles' only patch was the one for finishing the Iditarod twice before. Her fur hat didn't have anybody's name on it, though the style is known as a "Libby hat" because she made it herself. Libby makes and sells fur hats and other fur clothing, which is very popular among experienced mushers, and the profits pay for her own mushing.

There was great joy in Western Alaska when Libby won the race because she was the first Westerner to turn the trick. If that comes as a surprise to people who know Alaska well, it probably should. When it came time to start the 1982 Iditarod, there was no snow in Anchorage and the starting line had to be moved more than 50 miles northeast to Settlers Bay. Old timers up there say that Alaska doesn't really begin until you get well north of Anchorage. But even they have a healthy respect for the people and the animals who survive the weather out on Seward Peninsula, about one hundred miles down from the Arctic Circle.

This page: a snow-bound street in Nome, finishing point of the Iditarod. Facing page: Eagle Island.

Libby lives in an Eskimo village named Teller, a place she selected after having lived in several Alaskan towns since she arrived in the state at the age of sixteen. Her family, who live at the other end of the climatic scale in Phoenix, Arizona, all agree that she is a real "frontier type" for whom Alaska is absolutely perfect. The Alaskans proudly agree.

Libby Riddles was not among the people Alaskans particularly noticed in Anchorage on March 2, 1985. It was hard to notice anybody in that crowd of well-wishers and television crews and a thousand barking dogs. She had no corporate sponsors to give her a P.R. push, and she was 46th in the starting order of 62 teams. The rules allow as many as 18 dogs on a team, but Libby only

had 13, as if to mock the superstition already high in many circles in this 13th running of the Iditarod.

Most of the attention centered around Rick Mackey, who had won in 1983 and had run in more than half the races. Susan Butcher was another musher everyone had an eye out for. She had finished second twice and was in the top ten finalists six of

Crossing pack ice near Unalakleet. Facing page: McGrath.

Husky teams at rest, Anvik. Left and top left: Libby Riddles with Eskimo friends.

the seven times she has run the race. And, except for the sentimental favorite, "the father of the Iditarod," Joe Redington, the smart money was on Rick Swenson, out for his fifth win. If anybody had any money riding on Libby's chances, they had reasons of their own that most of the crowd didn't notice.

The 62 teams left Anchorage at two minute intervals in an order determined by lot. As has often happened, there was not enough snow on the streets to handle the sled traffic, so they imported some the night before. There was plenty outside the city limits, though, and the first leg of the race, a twenty mile run to Eagle River, was won be Susan Butcher who made it in two hours and three minutes. The run to the first checkpoint also produced the race's first casualty. Armen Khatchikian, the musher from Italy, was injured in a fall and had to call it quits with another 1,020 miles to go.

Susan was entitled to a thousand-dollar bonus prize for winning the first leg, but there was a catch: she had to finish the race to collect it. There was no reason to believe she wouldn't, but before the weekend was over, fate stepped in and Susan Butcher became the Iditarod's second casualty.

She was well in the lead on the race's first night and was taking advantage of clear weather conditions to get even further ahead. It had snowed the week before and the soft cover made

Facing page: derelict wooden building in the ghost-town of Iditarod.

A deserted Unalakleet scene. Top right: a young inhabitant of Anvik.

moving around a bit difficult. Iditarod volunteers had come through to mark the trail and the path they made took a lot of effort out of moving from place to place. The local moose considered that a great favor.

As Susan glided along, the soft snow deadening the sound, she reached the crest of the hill and suddenly found a moose right in her path. Before she could react, the moose attacked, killing one of her dogs and injuring two others. The moose kept them at bay for half an hour, kicking the dogs, breaking the lines and raising havoc. Finally help came in the form of musher Dewey Halverson who, unlike Susan, had a gun with him. It took four shots to dispatch the angry moose. But the help came too late for Susan's team. She dropped out of the race less than 200 miles out of Anchorage.

The rules of the race require that each musher carry an axe, but a gun is optional. More than one musher wished for one during that first day and night. More than 20 teams tangled with wandering moose. Some chose to go round them, making a new trail. But many were forced to stop and wait, losing valuable time. More than one moose was persuaded to move on after a rap on the head with an axe handle, but not every musher is willing to risk making a moose mad. Not

even with a $50,000 prize waiting in Nome.

By the third day, as they were beginning to climb the Alaska Mountain Range, everybody was beginning to show signs of the strain of two days and nights with little or no sleep. The rules demand that every musher takes one full 24-hour rest break, but when and where it should be done is a matter of personal preference. No one even considers a rest of more than an hour or two this early in the run. But in the

13th Iditarod, the trail in the early part of the race was soft with new-fallen snow. That meant it was not only slow but doubly tiring. It made a difference, but not a musher in the field was willing to give in to temptation to take a long winter's nap.

But, up ahead, Mother Nature was making up their mind for them. A heavy winter storm that forecasters promised would last at least three days was settling in over the mountains. Rainy pass, their projected route, was

This picture: on Knik Lake. Top left: veterinarians attend to an injured dog. Bottom left: on the Yukon River.

This page: McGrath. Facing page: satellite station on the shores of the frozen Bering Sea at Nome.

officially closed because of the danger of avalanches and the race officials tacked on a forty-mile detour to go around it. Everyone agreed that the Rainy Pass checkpoint was the place to take the required 24-hour break.

They didn't all arrive at the same time. The kind of thing that sometimes happens on fast turnpikes happened out in the snow-covered, lonely Happy Valley. There was a traffic pile-up. It all started when a sled slipped at the edge of a bluff, pulling dogs into the air and sending the sled into a snowbank. The musher, Ron Robbins, wound up in a tree. He had no sooner come back to his senses when Betsy McGuire's sled went over the same bluff, sending her into another snowbank. Then, minutes later, Joe Redington joined her as his team fell on top of her sled. Nearly three dozen mushers had accidents in the same spot. One lost two dogs and broke his right hand. Another wound up covered with the contents of a bucket of dog food all over himself and his sled.

The blame was placed at the feet of the trail-setters who were working fast after a snowstorm, but though mushers are a forgiving lot, most agreed the trail through Happy Valley was a good example of the difference between dogsleds and snow-mobiles. Dogs need more room to turn and can't go down hills that are so steep that the momentum of the sled catches up with them.

But there was no time for recriminations. The Iditarod mushers had other things to think about. The mountain storm was raging as predicted and it became impossible for airplanes to get through to the next checkpoint to drop vital food and supplies. Supply planes are never more than a day or so ahead of the first mushers because of the danger that wolves will steal the food before the dogs get there. It was possible to supply the east side of the mountain range, and so a decision was made to put the race on hold.

Before the race was suspended, the 58 mushers holed up at Rainy Pass were given the choice of sticking around for 24 hours or pushing forward into the storm that had already dumped two feet of new snow on the mountains. Though most seemed to favor continuing the race, none did. The men who ran the machines that set the trail were bogged down, too. Their snow-mobiles were out of gas. None of the mushers wanted to be the first through the deep snow, an act of charity to the others that would tire out the dogs and probably make the difference between winning and losing.

The race began again at ten o'clock on Wednesday night. By that time a ton and a half of ground meat and dog food had been airlifted in. The first mushers reached the next checkpoint at Rohn, 90 miles away, in just under 12 hours. They still had 900 miles to go. And another blizzard was in the weather forecast.

The route from Rainy Pass to Rohn skirts the south fork of the

Blizzard at Shaktoolik.

Kuskokwim River, the bane of many a musher because of its stretches of open water. It was there that veteran Joe Redington nearly found the end of the trail. Blinded by the glare on the ice, his team got caught in a strong cross-wind and was dumped into knee-deep freezing water. His sled was filled with water and so were his boots, and his dogs were badly shaken. Before he covered the next five miles to the next checkpoint, one of his dogs died.

When he arrived at the cabin that was the Rohn checkpoint, he dumped a quart of icy water from his boots.

These pages: McGrath.

The next checkpoint, ninety miles and another ten or twelve hours away, was the village of Nikolai, population 110. Everybody in town was out to greet the mushers, in spite of a howling arctic snowstorm. The youngest residents had to be there. They had an assignment from their teacher to collect the autograph of every musher who passed through town.

The storm at Nikolai was only the beginning of a string of them that would slow the race down over the next several days. By the ninth day, the race stopped again. It was the second time that had happened in the history of the race. It was also the second time in a week. This time, the problem was getting supplies into the ghost town of Iditarod, the place that gave its name to the trail.

Unlike the earlier suspension, not all the teams were at the same place when it went into effect. Some were at McGrath, a large town by interior Alaska's standards, but 26 were up ahead at Ophir. Because of complaints that the difference gave an unfair advantage to the 26, it was decided to restart them in staggered order based on their relative arrival time. Meanwhile,

Rick Swenson arrives in Nome.
Top right: entrant Fred Agree.

*Musher Monique Bene enters
Anvik. Facing page: aerial view of
the snaking Yukon River.*

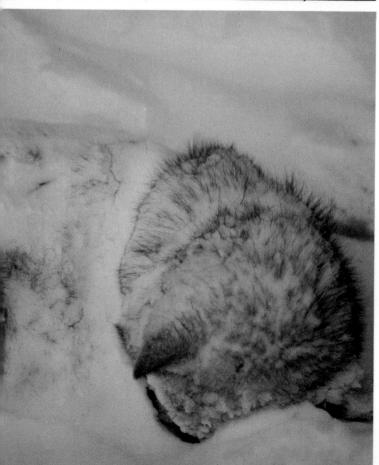

they were at the mercy of the weather. The storm dropped anywhere from 30 inches to six feet of snow on Western Alaska in ten days. The Iditarod Trail ran through areas of both extremes. People who had lived their entire lives in the Yukon River area said they had never seen that much snow. Every inch of new snow slows a dog team down. The dogs pick up balls of the stuff in their paws, mushers face the risk of falling into soft patches that are often waist-deep in spite of the fact that all of them carry snowshoes.

By the time the second suspension had lifted, after 36 hours, the race was already ten days old and there were still 650 miles to go.

If the mountains are tough, the rolling tundra can be worse. High winds and drifting snow covers the trail. But in the 1985 Iditarod, there was even worse ahead. By the time most of the mushers started the drive up the Yukon River, the temperature

Top left: a veterinarian with "patient."

had reached forty below zero. Even their eyelashes had ice balls on them. The dogs' fur was caked with ice. Veterans of Arctic winters knew that this was the time to break out high fat foods. Dogs were fed seal blubber, people ate sticks of butter like chocolate bars. It was a time to run behind the sleds to keep warm and be thankful for having worn the right combination of layers of clothing and insulation. It was a time when fatigue was the worst enemy. People get disoriented in such temperatures and more than one veteran musher was found near the Eagle Island checkpoint wandering aimlessly back and forth. Herbie Nayokpuk, one of the most seasoned of all the veterans, fell asleep on the next leg of the race and fell off his sled. His dogs made it to the checkpoint ten minutes ahead of him. Another competitor reported having run backwards for more than 40 miles to keep his back to the biting wind.

By the time they began the dash from the Yukon toward Norton Sound, a dozen teams were beginning to line themselves up for the final kill, and in spite of winds as high as 40 miles an hour, and below zero temperatures, nobody was giving much thought to resting.

What had been an endurance contest was beginning to look like a race. By the time the first dozen teams pulled into Unalakleet, 270 miles from the finish line, Lavon Barve was the front-runner. Libby Riddles was two hours behind him. But she was first out, taking the first step in her big gamble. Her team, driven by her friend Joe Garnie, had finished second the year before, and though they were worn out, she knew they had the right stuff. She was out to prove that she did, too.

By the time she reached the next checkpoint, a blizzard driven by winds of more than 30 miles an hour was howling across the ice on Norton Bay, which was

where the trail would take her next. She would have a three-hour head start on Lavon Barve if she left right away. The next eleven mushers were right behind him.

But if she left right away, it would be a rough, 58-mile drive across the ice. Libby Riddles took the chance. There were times when she could see nothing but white. Ten-foot snowdrifts became almost invisible. The wind in her face made any thought of seeing the trail markers impossible. But she made it to the Eskimo Village of Shaktoolik, where one of the first people she met told her that in the windy season in January, people have to crawl on the ground to get anywhere without being blown over. More consolation than that was that she had established a good lead. "Those guys behind me are going to have to go through worse wind," she said. "And I hope they suffer for it, nice person that I am."

But she wasn't so nice as to wait and greet them. She was gone before any of them arrived. Twenty-four hours later she was 60 miles closer to Nome, with pack ice and a raging windstorm behind her. Six of her competitors were out there, but nowhere in sight. She could sympathize with them. During the previous night, blowing snow had concealed all the markers and she was forced to park her sled. That meant changing from her wet clothes and getting into a sleeping bag. She knew she would not move again until morning. Even then moving wasn't easy. But nobody said winning the Iditarod was easy.

By the 18th day of the race Libby Riddles had a five-hour lead and 77 miles to go. By that point, the field had shifted quite a bit and her nearest competitor was Dewey Halverson, the man who shot the moose for Susan Butcher two and a half weeks before. He and Libby Riddles had learnt how to handle a dog sled together ten years before.

As she left the White Mountain checkpoint for the last dash, she was able to say, "I'm just going to take it easy the rest of the way. I don't want to make everybody get up too early."

She was met by several hundred people the next day after mushing all night. Not one of them complained about having to get up too early.